Issues Related to Parenting

Issues Related to Parenting

By J. Luke Martin

Rod and Staff Publishers, Inc.
Crockett, Kentucky 41413

Copyright 1995
by
Rod and Staff Publishers, Inc.
Crockett, Kentucky 41413

Code no. 95-2-96

Contents

1. Practical Helps in Relating to Children 9
2. Preparation for Training 13
3. The Value and Potential of the Child 17
4. The Child a Threefold Being 23
5. The Child's First Years 33
6. The Discipline of the Child 39
7. Character Development 45

"And they brought young children to him, that he should touch them: and his disciples rebuked those that brought them. But when Jesus saw it, he was much displeased, and said unto them, Suffer the little children to come unto me, and forbid them not: for of such is the kingdom of God. Verily I say unto you, Whosoever shall not receive the kingdom of God as a little child, he shall not enter therein."

Mark 10:13-15

1.

Practical Helps in Relating to Children

Children are not born to seasoned, experienced grandparents, but to inexperienced—and sometimes young and immature—parents. We believe that God has a definite purpose for this. Jesus said, "Without me ye can do nothing"—that is, nothing of any value or spiritual significance. Our success and effectiveness as Christian parents will depend primarily on our dependency upon and commitment

Issues Related to Parenting

to Jesus Christ as our teacher, example, and source of wisdom.

The Bible gives us insights into godly homes such as Abraham and Sarah's, Amram and Jochebed's, Elkanah and Hannah's, Mordecai and Esther's, and Lois, Eunice, and Timothy's. It also exposes the failure and weaknesses of homes like Eli's, David's, and Solomon's. We can learn something from all of them.

The Bible does not provide an outlined, detailed, step-by-step procedure to follow in training a child from day one to the age of twenty-one. It does give various principles that, if faithfully followed, will establish credibility and ensure God's blessing.

The New Testament assumes that godly parents will endeavor to raise and nurture their children in a godly way. "And, ye fathers, provoke not your children to wrath: but *bring them up* in the nurture and admonition of the Lord" (Ephesians 6:4). One qualification for a church leader is that he rule well his own

Practical Helps in Relating to Children

house, having his children in subjection with all gravity. (See 1 Timothy 3:4, 12; Titus 1:6.)

"And these words, which I command thee this day, shall be in thine heart: and thou shalt teach them diligently unto thy children, and shalt talk of them when thou sittest in thine house, and when thou walkest by the way, and when thou liest down, and when thou risest up."

Deuteronomy 6:6, 7

2.

Preparation for Training

The apostle Paul admonishes in 1 Timothy 5:14 that "the younger women marry, bear children, guide the house, give none occasion to the adversary to speak reproachfully." Such a responsibility calls for much consideration.

Theodore Roosevelt once said, "The task of motherhood and fatherhood, the task of providing for the home and keeping it, is the greatest fundamental task of humanity. If

Issues Related to Parenting

Mother does not do *her duty*, there will either be *no* next generation or a generation that is *worse* than none at all."

1. Prospective parents need to seek the face of God as Manoah and his wife did. "Then Manoah intreated the Lord, and said, O my Lord, let the man of God which thou didst send come again unto us, and *teach* us what we shall do unto the child that shall be born" (Judges 13:8).

2. Prospective parents also need to consider that giving birth to children is much more than a physical accomplishment. Spiritual powers are at work, and eternal destinies are involved.

3. Husband and wife need to communicate with each other concerning the specific details and values that are important in the nurture of children. Then they need to decide how they can best implement these convictions.

4. Prospective parents need to consider that they will transmit an Adamic nature to

Preparation for Training

their child. As the child develops, his inborn selfish nature will become pronounced. As it does, the parents' personal example of a spiritual transformation by the grace of God is of critical importance.

5. Prospective parents will want to participate actively in a spiritual fellowship of believers. There is no such thing as perfect parents. With the best of intentions and commitment, areas of weakness and blindness will exist. The combined strengths of a variety of homes, blended together in a spiritual fellowship, provide the greatest potential for success.

"The Lord is nigh unto all them that call upon him, to all that call upon him in truth. He will fulfil the desire of them that fear him: he also will hear their cry, and will save them."

Psalm 145:18, 19

3.

The Value and Potential of the Child

All adults began as innocent infants. Only as infants grow to maturity and begin to make choices are destinies determined. Just think of influential men of the recent past. Adolf Hitler and Daniel Kauffman both started life as innocent babies, but, oh, what contrasts they were by the end of their lives! What part did training or the lack of it contribute to their destinies?

Issues Related to Parenting

1. *The Struggle Between God and Satan for the Child*

We believe that next to God, Satan knows best the potential of a godly seed. The scene in Revelation 12 pictures Satan ready to devour the Christ-child at His birth. Certainly Almighty God's intervention should provide young parents with a tremendous anchor of faith that the same deliverance is available for their own children.

But bear in mind that just as Satan sought to destroy the Christ-child from birth, he will seek to destroy the seed of every godly parent, not necessarily physically, but rather spiritually through a subtle, diabolical scheme of "innocent" tolerance, negligence, and compromise on the part of the parents themselves.

Consider some Bible examples. God promised Abraham that through his seed all the families of the earth would be blest. This was a prophetic message concerning Jesus Christ. Working through Pharaoh, Satan decreed that every male Hebrew infant be cast into

The Value and Potential of the Child

the Nile River. But praise God, one home refused to cooperate with Satan's plan.

Later God promised David that of his seed there would arise a King who would reign forever. Again we see Satan working through wicked Athaliah, who determined to destroy all the *seed* royal. Again his plan was thwarted. Faithful Jehosheba rescued Joash and hid him.

Lastly we see Satan making a last-ditch effort through King Herod to destroy the Christ-child of Bethlehem. Yet He who was the promised seed of the woman was divinely preserved. Just so, there is also hope for every child whose parents seek the face of God and follow His command.

2. *Spiritual Lessons of Childhood*

Someone once asked the question "Why was it necessary for Jesus to come as a babe?" The answer came back: "Because that is the only way we can come to Him." So it is. Jesus said that except we become as *little* children, we *cannot enter* the kingdom of heaven. While

Issues Related to Parenting

the human mind cannot comprehend the full purposes of God in the Incarnation, certainly this aspect is one vital truth concerning it.

In Isaiah's time of gloom and doom, the hope of Israel did not lie in a full-grown man, but in a child (Isaiah 7:14). In 9:6 the child again appears as the one who will be the ultimate ruler, not only of Israel but of all the redeemed. Again, in chapter 11 it is the child who is the pictured emblem of Christ's kingdom of peace. In the child all God's purposes lie latent. As children come to maturity, God's purposes begin to be realized, provided that the child has been given the proper training and of his own volition makes right choices.

Paul admonished the Corinthians, "In malice be ye children, but in understanding be men" (1 Corinthians 14:20). Children forgive and forget their childish disagreements very easily. As adults, we should learn a lesson from them. With the understanding of men we should choose the way of forgiveness and learn its eternal value.

Children's Prayer

In the early morning when the sunbeams bright
    Shine around our pathway, scattering the night,
Jesus, gentle Saviour, hear our earnest prayer;
    Bless the little children, take us in Thy care.

When temptations gather, fears or foes affright,
    When our footsteps waver in the path of right,
Jesus, tender Saviour, with Thine arm uphold;
    All our upward strivings in Thy love enfold.

When the shadows lengthen, bringing sweet repose,
    Weary hands are folded, little eyelids close,
Jesus, loving Saviour, guard us thro' the night;
    Keep Thy little children safe till morning light.

"And the child grew, and waxed strong in spirit, filled with wisdom: and the grace of God was upon him . . . And he said unto them, How is it that ye sought me? Wist ye not that I must be about my Father's business?"

Luke 2:40, 49

4.

The Child a Threefold Being

The Bible speaks of man as a threefold being—spirit, soul, and body. Infants are that at birth, yet parents tend naturally to concentrate primarily on the nurture of the body. The infant is fed, clothed, and sheltered with the best of care.

1. The Child's Spirit
In Genesis 2:7 we read, "The Lord God formed man . . . and breathed into his

Issues Related to Parenting

nostrils the breath of life; and man became a living soul." The spirit of the child is the very life of the child. It is also that inner consciousness by which the child comes to know himself as a person. It is within the child's spirit that he develops a consciousness of God and all other personalities.

Through his spirit the child senses acceptance or rejection, tension or rest, love or animosity, happiness or sadness. The child is sensitive to these emotions very early, long before he or she can talk or communicate.

Ministering to a child's spirit should become a primary goal of every sincere parent and should begin even before birth. Women who are frustrated and resentful of their calling are already sending a negative signal to the unborn. Parents who argue and quarrel or speak harshly are also conveying a message. In contrast, parents who trust, pray, sing, and communicate with each other in love provide an atmos-

The Child a Threefold Being

phere of rest that gives the unborn a tremendous advantage.

Perhaps a hospital experiment will help us to more readily comprehend these facts. A certain hospital that specializes in prenatal care played soft music and hymns to a control group of premature babies. A second group heard no music. The first group gained considerably faster. There was also a third group for which they played *rock* music. The hospital soon had to abandon this experiment because these infants began to lose weight and became very colicky.

Infants whose mothers cuddle them and who call them often by their own name have been proven to respond to other stimuli at a more rapid rate than infants who do not receive such attentions. Coupling this with reading Bible stories and singing children's lullabies over and over again brings an unspoken comfort and security to the infant's spirit, even before he or she can articulate words.

2. The Child's Soul

The terms *spirit* and *soul* are sometimes used interchangeably in the Bible and refer to the same thing. Yet in definition we distinguish the soul as the very character of the individual as expressed in the intellect, the emotions, and the will.

Parents look forward with keen anticipation to the development of their newborn infant's understanding. That first smile, the particular noticing of bright objects, the first semblance of syllables that sound like Mama or Papa (Dad) are met with great delight. Parents who give studied attention to help a young child develop his intellect at a very young age contribute both to his capacity to learn and to his ability to grasp facts when he enters school. This requires intentional communication.

Showing him an object such as a ball or a baby in a book and then asking him to identify it helps the young child begin to make rational decisions. Reading the same

The Child a Threefold Being

story over and over, particularly a Bible story with pictures, and then asking questions about the various illustrations in the picture stimulates the child's mind. This routine should begin before the child can talk. It teaches him to think.

A child expresses his feelings through emotion. The wise parent will pay attention to the child's cry or laughter. An infant usually cries when he is hungry or in pain. It may be he has some other discomfort or senses fear. Discerning the reason for an infant's continued crying is not always easy. Sometimes the cry reflects the tensions of a tired nursing mother.

As the infant grows a little older, he may cry because of anger over some discomfort. At this juncture the infant may be too small to spank, yet a firm hold and a gentle "no, no" registers a mental impression on his spirit. Consistently following this pattern at an early stage teaches the child that the emotions must also be controlled. It is right to let the child cry for a short time after he is corrected,

Issues Related to Parenting

but continuous crying that ends in pouting calls for more correction.

Closely related to the emotions is the child's will. Every child is born with an Adamic nature that will very early express itself in selfishness. The young child knows only his own interests. He could not care less about another's hunger, feelings, or desires. The child's will demands that his needs and desires be satisfied right now. While immediate gratification may be necessary at the start, it is good to bring the child into a routine schedule in order to teach him that his will needs to be subject to order and discipline. The more consistently this is done, the easier it will be for the child to learn the blessing of other boundaries that his parents establish.

A child must be taught very early that he must submit his will to the will of his parents. The parent decides which toys are allowed and when, the play area, and how the toys must be shared with other siblings

The Child a Threefold Being

if there are any. It is for the parents to decide when candy may be eaten and how much. Invariably the child's will will run counter to these restrictions. Yet it is in these small, seemingly easily overlooked issues that indelible impressions are made on the intellect, emotions, and will of the child.

3. The Child's Body

God created man with a visible physical body. It is this living physical body that becomes the joy of the new mother and father when the first cry of life issues forth from the infant's lips.

The infant is born unclothed. One of the first efforts of the parent is to clothe the newborn and then to proceed to give nourishment. This was true of Mary, the mother of the Christ-child. "And she brought forth her firstborn son, and wrapped him in swaddling clothes" (Luke 2:7).

This inborn, natural response to clothe and feed the body can become a snare that

Issues Related to Parenting

Satan can and has used to trap many well-meaning parents. Mothers especially not only see the necessity to clothe their children, but also yield to the temptation to doll them up. Such a temptation is very subtle. The parents, instead of conscientiously giving precedence to the nurture of the child's spirit and soul, concentrate on his physical development and appearance. Jesus' question in Matthew 6:25 strikes to the core of this issue. "Is not the life more than meat, and the body than raiment?"

Why is the outward adorning of the body a continuous issue among Christian people? Does not the answer lie in the fact that many fathers and mothers have succumbed to the temptation that it is acceptable to lavish their pride and secret love for bodily adornment on their children? Accenting bodily adornment over and above character development establishes in a child's mentality a precedent that becomes deeply rooted. Satan would have it so.

The Child a Threefold Being

Conscientious parents will see that their children are properly fed and clothed. Yet their paramount concern is the nurture and development of the child's spirit and character. We believe that it was so in Jesus' home. The result was that Jesus grew in wisdom and stature and in favor with God and man.

Children who are taught to keep the body in subjection to spiritual law make a greater and better contribution to the church than those taught otherwise. The ones who become enslaved to bodily adornment *smother* their usefulness in the kingdom.

"By faith Moses, when he was come to years, refused to be called the son of Pharaoh's daughter; choosing rather to suffer affliction with the people of God, than to enjoy the pleasures of sin for a season; esteeming the reproach of Christ greater riches than the treasures in Egypt: for he had respect unto the recompence of the reward. By faith he forsook Egypt, not fearing the wrath of the king: for he endured, as seeing him who is invisible."

Hebrews 11:24-27

5.

The Child's First Years

The Biblical account in Hebrews 11 of Moses' understanding and the choices he made when he came to maturity is simply amazing. Taken from his parental home at a very young age and thrust into the culture and learning of pagan Egypt, he nevertheless maintained some valuable truth. The martyr Stephen said that Moses was learned in all the wisdom of Egypt and was mighty

Issues Related to Parenting

in words and deeds (Acts 7:22).

According to the account in Hebrews 11:24–27, Moses (1) knew who the people of God really were; (2) understood that while sin may offer some physical pleasure, it only lasts for a season; (3) knew and believed about the coming Messiah; (4) correctly evaluated that heavenly rewards are of greater value than earthly treasure; (5) knew that the invisible God could protect him from the anger of a powerful earthly king; and (6) possessed the character to do what was right, regardless of what it cost him.

He did all this by faith. Romans 10:17 says that "faith cometh by hearing." Where did Moses hear? He certainly did not acquire faith from a Bible in Pharaoh's library! No, he heard these valuable eternal truths from the lips of his mother and father. He must have heard them over and over at a very young age. His parents had a vision.

We do not believe that children are capable of experiencing Scriptural conversion (the

The Child's First Years

New Birth) at a very young age (in child evangelism), but we do believe in Biblical nurture. It is important and right that we fill the child's mind with all the *facts* of truth that the child is capable of absorbing.

A teacher of first grade students had the policy of quizzing beginners on their knowledge of simple Bible stories. Such a survey was often disheartening. Many pupils were ignorant of who the first people were who lived on the earth. Some seemingly had never heard about Noah and the flood, Joseph, or Daniel. This is a serious indictment against the parents of these children.

Parents take too much for granted. They assume that little children will just catch on. But the Bible commands that they be taught. We live in a fast-moving society, but nothing should ever replace the bedtime Bible story, prayer, and the routine schedule of teaching small children the moral law of right behavior.

The one supreme fact that should be

Issues Related to Parenting

indelibly impressed on the small child's mind is that of God. It is God who gives us food and clothes. It is God who created the beautiful world and makes the sun to shine and sends the rain. It is God who heals injuries and makes sick people well. It is God we adore and worship when we gather for the public meeting. It is to God they say their bedtime prayers before climbing into bed.

This is not trying to make "little Christians" out of our children. It is simply establishing within them a consciousness that Father and Mother love God and that God loves them all. It also establishes a consciousness that everything and every person has meaning because God is the supreme Creator. Certainly children are not able to define these truths, but the facts must be taught in order to provide them with a proper foundation on which to build their developing powers of understanding.

In Our Dear Lord's Garden

In our dear Lord's garden,
    Planted here below,
Many tiny flowers
    In sweet beauty grow.

Jesus loves the children,
    Children such as we;
Blest them when their mothers
    Brought them to His knee.

Lord, Thy call we answer;
    Take us in Thy care;
Train us in Thy garden
    In Thy works to share.

Nothing is too little
    For His gentle care;
Nothing is too lowly
    In His love to share.

"For whom the Lord loveth he chasteneth, and scourgeth every son whom he receiveth. If ye endure chastening, God dealeth with you as with sons; for what son is he whom the father chasteneth not? . . . Now no chastening for the present seemeth to be joyous, but grievous: nevertheless afterward it yieldeth the peaceable fruit of righteousness unto them which are exercised thereby."

Hebrews 12:6, 7, 11

6.

The Discipline of the Child

Discipline is often thought of as corporal punishment, such as spanking or any other form of physical correction. Such action is corrective discipline administered for disobedience. But parents should consider discipline more in terms of *prevention* than in terms of *correction.* This does not minimize the need for correction, but preventive discipline springs from a mother and a father's

Issues Related to Parenting

love that communicates very early the valuable lesson that obedience brings happiness—not only to the child, but even more so to the parents.

As well as teaching the child what is right, parents must also express delight and pleasure for obedience. This does not mean rewarding a child for every detailed act of obedience, but simply expressing an attitude of appreciation for the child's efforts. Doing so establishes a relationship and a bond of love between parent and child. Only when this bond of love exists can corrective discipline be effective. As the child matures, he begins to understand that the punishment hurts his parents nearly as much as himself.

Corrective discipline without a love relationship tends to develop bitterness in the heart. When a parent allows bitterness to enter his heart, distance develops between parent and child, and unless stopped, this distance will increase. At the point where such a situation becomes evident, the wise

The Discipline of the Child

parent will humble himself before the Lord in repentance and seek forgiveness and deliverance.

Discipline is most effective when it is consistent. To be strict one day and lenient the next sends the child confusing signals. The child will not only become confused, but frustrated as well. Children perform best when they know what is expected and what will be required.

Along with being consistent, a parent must avoid nagging. Scolding and shaming may have their place, but constant nagging will only harden the child and destroy the bond of love. Rather, a command that is authoritative, without leaving any option except obedience, will go a long way in helping the child develop a right sense of responsibility.

The father is normally the one responsible to establish discipline in the life of each child. We believe that the father will be held responsible for what is allowed. But the role of the mother as she enters into and supports

Issues Related to Parenting

disciplinary training of the child cannot be overestimated. Proverbs 1:8 and 6:20 speak of the "law" of the mother in conjunction with the father's instruction and commandment.

This law of the mother is the firm conviction of moral responsibility that compels her to duty. It is the exact opposite of the flippant, permissive, indulgent attitude characteristic of many mothers today. Mothers who have established law pay close attention to small details. They guard very carefully the child's actions and reactions. These include the way the child plays with his toys and with others, as well as the child's eating habits. Children need to be taught to eat what is set before them and to clean up their plates. Mothers also need to be concerned with the way their children relate to their bodies by keeping themselves covered and modest. Her law also relates to the way the child responds to the commands to come and to stop.

It is the mother who is most constantly

The Discipline of the Child

with the child in the early years. She is the one who will register the early impressions of acceptance and expectation upon the child's consciousness. It is she who will most often inflict those early punishments. Blessed are those children indeed who have a mother who fears God and seeks to guide their little feet in right paths.

The father is responsible to support and encourage the mother in fulfilling her role, which completes the structure of discipline. It is imperative that parents be united in their purpose and methods of discipline. Parents should privately discuss together the methods they use and evaluate their effectiveness. Sometimes fathers are lax in their duty and need gentle reminders from Mother. Or perhaps a mother becomes weary of the task and needs encouragement from Father. It is a fact that the sterner, more severe chastenings given by the father will bring the child to rest and will reduce the need for Mother to become weary of the task.

"And Eli perceived that the Lord had called the child. Therefore Eli said unto Samuel, Go lie down: and it shall be, if he call thee, that thou shalt say, Speak, Lord; for thy servant heareth. So Samuel went and lay down in his place. And the Lord came, and stood, and called as at other times, Samuel, Samuel. Then Samuel answered, Speak; for thy servant heareth."

1 Samuel 3:8-10

7.

Character Development

The word *character* does not appear in the Bible. However, the words *integrity* (in the Old Testament) and *virtue* (in the New Testament) have the same basic meaning. "The integrity of the upright shall guide them: but the perverseness of transgressors shall destroy them" (Proverbs 11:3).

Integrity simply means an upright life, being the same all the way through, and the ability to control oneself in a time of crisis. Good character has been defined as the ability to recognize what is right, kind, decent, wise, and loving in every situation; having the desire to do these things; and acting consistently in accordance with this knowledge and desire.

Character in general includes all of a person's qualities or features; it is the prevailing nature of a person or thing. It involves moral strength or weakness. The special ways in which any person feels, thinks, or acts, whether they be good or bad, make up his character. Good character therefore is the expression of moral firmness and self-control.

Proper character development is important if we want to ensure a good foundation for congenial relationships in the home. Good character is an asset and provides a safeguard that helps the child cope with peer pressure. It is youth with sound character who come through the crisis experiences of life successfully. This is especially true when their lives are subjected to the control of the Holy Spirit.

Character Development

Parents bear the primary responsibility for the development of proper character. Good character does not develop spontaneously. Children have to be taught what is right and then be required to do it consistently.

When we really get serious about building character into the lives of our children, we may need to go through a school of rehabilitation ourselves. Why? Because the deficiencies we see in our children probably reflect our own. Some parents are blind to their children's character deficiencies because they are blind to their own. Within a church body of faithful believers such a situation will be less likely to develop if parents are open to the counsel and observation of others.

Let us consider a number of specific character traits.

1. Attentiveness

Attentiveness is the trait of listening carefully to the one who is speaking. Being attentive causes a person to be alert to those from

Issues Related to Parenting

whom he can learn. It helps one to be sensitive to others who may be in need of help. Attentiveness is an absolute necessity for learning both obedience and safety.

Children who enter first grade and have not been trained to be attentive will be seriously handicapped. The child who does not listen to instructions cannot follow them. If he does not listen to the lesson as it is explained, he will not learn.

The Scriptures provide us with a vivid example of a child who was taught to listen explicitly. First Samuel 3:2–10 gives the account of God's calling to Samuel in the dark hours of the night. Samuel responded immediately. Supposing that Eli the priest was calling, he quickly ran to Eli's room to see what Eli wanted. After the third repetition of this occurrence, Eli told Samuel to say, "Speak, Lord; for thy servant heareth." How many of our children would respond with such persistent obedience?

The child who has been trained to be sensitive to his parents and others when they

Character Development

speak to him will be better able to discern the call of the Holy Spirit when he comes to the age of spiritual accountability. Romans 10:17 says, "Faith cometh by hearing, and hearing by the word of God." The child who has not been taught to listen to the voice of authority will have a difficult time coming to the faith.

Hebrews 2:1 says that we should "give the more earnest heed to the things which we have heard, lest at any time we should let them slip." Revelation 2:7 says, "He that hath an ear, let him hear what the Spirit saith unto the churches." These and many other Scriptures speak to the necessity of paying close attention. Doing so just might make all the difference in our eternal destiny.

To develop good attentiveness, start early to speak directly to your infant. Call him by name and respond to his responses. Require him to stop whatever he is doing when he is spoken to. Be satisfied with nothing less than an answer, at least a yes or a no. A shrug of

Issues Related to Parenting

the shoulders should not be accepted as an answer. Test your child occasionally by having him repeat what you have said. Once a child is attentive, he is ready to learn to obey.

2. Obedience

True obedience entails doing what an authority figure asks us to do. It means doing it immediately, respectfully, joyfully, and completely. It is the opposite of doing our own thing.

Obedience requires the submission of the child's will to those who are in charge. The child must be taught this submission through the process of love and law. Because the child's will is set to do his own thing, he must be taught very early the meaning of the little word *no*. To learn this, he will of necessity experience pain and correction. Disobedience should always be understood to equal pain, suffering, and regret. Of course, the opposite will also be true: obedience brings happiness, approval, and satisfaction.

Character Development

Obedience should have top priority in the parent's scale of values. No one can experience salvation apart from obedience. It is God who commands us to obey Him first of all. He also commands that we obey those to whom He has delegated authority, such as government officials, church leaders, and the boss on the job. Obedience is essential if the child is to attain to his highest usefulness in God's kingdom.

Obedience helps children to see love behind authority. As long as a child is allowed to challenge authority, he will see only what the authority is denying or requiring. Both he and the parents will be unhappy. Once the child is taught to submit his will promptly, he will be able to come to rest in his spirit and respect (i.e., see the authority and wisdom of) discipline. He then will be able to enjoy the protection and security that come from being under authority.

To teach obedience effectively, the parents should seriously consider their own obedience.

Issues Related to Parenting

Does the child see you bowing before the authority of heaven as you face your responsibilities? Does he see you going to the Word of God for direction? Do you consistently obey those who are called to shepherd the flock of God? Expecting wholehearted obedience from the child is futile if our own obedience is in question.

Teaching obedience requires that the parent be reasonable. He can require only what is within the child's understanding and ability to comprehend and perform. What is required must not go beyond safe boundary lines so that the child can come to realize that his parents have his best interests in mind. Consistency in this process, coupled with daily communication, will rivet indelible impressions and establish a mutual relationship between parent and child.

3. Contentment

Discontentment, which is inherent in the nature of children, means dissatisfaction with their present state and condition. It is

Character Development

an inner response to the things they see but have not obtained, such as another child's toys or possibly something they saw pictured in a catalog or displayed on a store shelf. It may also involve things that other children are allowed to do but that they themselves are forbidden to do.

Billions of dollars are spent each year on advertisements that promote discontentment. Newer, bigger, and supposedly better items are paraded before our eyes to make us dissatisfied with what we have. The covetous heart is appealed to in such a way that idolatry becomes a real threat.

Only the child who has learned contentment is happy. To accomplish this, the child's basic needs must be met. He must be nourished with a sufficient diet, he must have clothing appropriate to the climate, and he must be surrounded by love.

When these basic requirements have been met, parents should proceed by their example to demonstrate to the child that "things" do not bring happiness. The child must be taught that God is in absolute control of all things and that He has promised to provide for us all that is essential. The child must learn to feel gratitude each day for the little things of life and to enjoy them.

Children can be taught at an early age to amuse themselves by *creating* rather than by *getting*. Building structures from wooden blocks or putting simple puzzles together stimulates the mind more than the modern electronic toy that is already obsolete when the battery dies.

Contentment needs to be taught in relation to basic needs. It is important that the child learn to eat what he is served. He should not be allowed to decide his own menu. He must be taught which foods are essential for good health and then be required to eat them.

Children who are taught to be content with the necessities of life will be better able to cope with the temptation to become possessive and materialistic when they see their

Character Development

peers indulging in extravagance. Contentment will later help them to live a life of discipleship, which is nothing less than giving up all for the sake of Christ.

4. Neatness and Orderliness

The child is born into a confused and disorderly society. But God is not the author of confusion. He is a God of order. The whole universe functions according to His exact timing. It is sin that brings disorder.

Orderliness and neatness need to be taught and inspired. Children are not very old before they unconsciously develop concepts of order or disorder. Having a set bedtime and a regular time to get up in the morning is important. Encourage and insist that proper attention be given to personal grooming, such as washing face and hands, combing the hair, and regular bathing. Having scheduled mealtimes also enhances orderliness.

Orderliness and neatness have also been defined as preparing oneself and one's

Issues Related to Parenting

surroundings to achieve the greatest efficiency. How true! Just think of how much time is saved when there is a place for everything and everything is put in its place. Small things like putting away toys, making beds, caring for clothing, and putting away shoes and boots are jobs that small children can do.

Jesus, when feeding the five thousand, left us a timeless example. He had everyone seated in orderly fashion. After everyone had eaten, what remained was carefully gathered up. Order contributes to economy.

5. Reverence and Respect

Reverence is a deep respect for God, for others, and for oneself. The little child should be taught very early to think of God with esteem because He is the highest Authority. As the child's understanding continues to mature, this esteem should develop into a wonder mixed with love and fear. A proper reverence for God will also produce respect for those to whom God has delegated responsibility

Character Development

to teach knowledge and wisdom. Those authorities are you, his parents, the Sunday and day school teacher, the pastor, the employer, civil officers, and anyone else who is commissioned to maintain order.

Children who are not taught to respect others usually develop little regard for themselves or their peers. They will not care for their own appearance, dress, or speech. Besides manifesting unkindness and discourtesy for others, such children often fall into abuse of their own bodies and persons.

Lack of respect for others causes real problems for the teacher when the child starts school. It also affects discipline. Disrespect lies at the heart of many of the academic difficulties children experience. This is explained in the proverb "The fear of the Lord is the beginning of knowledge: but fools despise wisdom and instruction" (Proverbs 1:7).

Respect should be given to the property of other people as well as to their persons. All property is owned by someone whom

Issues Related to Parenting

God has made. When children are allowed to abuse or destroy another's property, they to some extent destroy the owner's well-being and rob God by doing so.

By their attitudes and behavior, parents very early convey a sense of reverence or the lack of it. Parents who lose their temper, raise their voices, or holler and scream at their children place those children at a tremendous disadvantage. Unless a sincere apology is made when this happens and an effort made to relate honorably, permanent damage will be done to the child's spirit. In contrast, parents who demonstrate appreciation for each other and for others—their in-laws, pastors, teachers, employers, and neighbors—plant seeds of proper respect in the child's frame of reference.

Parents should strictly forbid teasing, belittling people, jesting, and gossiping. The saying "If you can't speak well of a person, you should not speak at all" is worth practicing. Conversely, the use of honorary titles,

Character Development

such as brother and sister, aunt and uncle, sir and madam, will establish a sense of relationship that enhances appreciation for authority.

6. Forgiveness

Teaching and helping your child to learn forgiveness are essential to sound character development. Forgiveness is the voluntary choice to pardon, excuse, and forget others' wrongs against us. It is the full heartfelt release of any bitterness or resentment aroused against someone who trespassed against us. It requires relinquishing every desire to get even or to return the hurt.

Forgiveness also involves confession and restitution on the part of the individual who hurts and offends another. The child must learn not only to forgive others, but also to seek forgiveness by making confession, apology, and restitution when he wrongs them.

Unforgiving attitudes are the cause of many home relationship problems. Parents who fail

Issues Related to Parenting

to deal redemptively with their child's disobedience by correction and forgiveness immediately place a wall between themselves and their child. Guilt and negative attitudes that are not brought out into the open, cleared up, and forgiven will fester like hidden sores and will continue to erupt and worsen with time.

Children must be taught and shown by parental example that confessing wrongdoing is honorable and right. Every child should be privileged to hear his father and mother say, "I'm sorry." Children must also witness the peace that forgiveness brings when pardon is expressed and the matter forever closed and forgotten. To dig up the past or to rehearse offenses that have been properly cleared does a terrible injustice to any child.

The child who cannot feel forgiveness will not learn to forgive others either. Thus begins a course of life that will lead to many strained and broken relationships. Children run away from home, marriage partners divorce, youth turn to rock music and drugs, all in efforts

Character Development

to escape the condemnation that comes from guilt that is not cleared and forgiven.

The Lord Jesus set the example for forgiveness. When hanging and suffering on the cruel cross, He looked down in pity upon His persecutors and said, "Father, forgive them; for they know not what they do." We who have received forgiveness from God will forfeit that forgiveness if from our hearts we do not forgive our brothers their trespasses (Matthew 18:35). Children need the assurance of their parents' forgiveness. They also need the example of parents who refuse to hold any accounts against another even if they have been hurt or offended by that person's thoughtlessness.

7. Honesty and Truthfulness

Without being truthful, a person will never be able to seek from God and others and to enjoy the forgiveness that depends on truthfully acknowledging the need to be forgiven. Without truthfulness a person is doomed to having his word questioned and scrutinized—or simply ignored—even when he is telling the truth.

To escape the tragedy of living a life of deception later, a child must learn to be truthful from his early years onward. Truthfulness is a way of earning future trust by accurately reporting facts and events. A child needs to learn to gain the approval of others without misrepresenting the facts. For a child to be truthful, he must be taught to face the consequences of mistakes. Lying to avoid punishment will lead to other distortions of character and moral ruin.

The child must learn that truthfulness must start with *me*. Unless a child can be completely honest with himself, he will never be able to accept himself as he is. Without truthfulness he will never be able to seek help to strengthen the weak areas in his life, because he will not be able to face his needs honestly.

Being completely honest with oneself is a most difficult step. But it must be taken

Character Development

and followed by a determination to be totally and completely honest with God and others. Unless he is truthful, the child will grow up making excuses for himself, covering up, and exaggerating. He will isolate himself from others by a wall of falsehoods and distortions that he erects to hide behind. He will live with the constant fear that the lies he told to avoid the consequences of mistakes and failures will be exposed.

Teach the child early that "lying lips are abomination to the Lord: but they that deal truly are his delight" (Proverbs 12:22). Make your own life an example of truthfulness. Tell the truth when you are questioned about possible errors you may be guilty of, such as missing prayer meeting because something else seemed more important at the time. Be honest with your child and apologize when you misjudge or falsely accuse him.

Reduce punishments for offenses when the child tells the truth immediately after being caught in wrongdoing. Let your child know that an honest confession is always more honorable than lying in order to escape consequences. Praise truthfulness. Let your child know how happy it makes you when the truth is told.

Above all, start early to teach what the Bible says about truthfulness and the evils of lying. Read stories about characters who were honest and refused to lie even though doing so sometimes seemed costly. Let your child know what the end of all liars will be (Revelation 21:7, 8) in contrast to the reward of those who are truthful.

8. Faith

Helping your child to develop a proper faith is another essential in building sound character. Faith in its simplest form is simply trusting someone to do what he has promised to do, or believing what is said on the basis of confidence without any other proof.

No child will develop a healthy character unless he has learned to trust his parents and believe what they tell him. The child's belief

Character Development

in God, in Creation, in history, and in his future teachers will depend largely on the degree of faith that he learns to have in his parents.

"Faith cometh by hearing" (Romans 10:17). The child who hears his parents repeat Scriptures or appeal to them for answers to the perplexities of life will develop a subconscious faith in this resource. Hearing you as a parent call upon God in prayer or praise and sensing that you love and obey the unseen God will furnish him with enough proof of the existence of the eternal God.

Faith is essential to the child's future salvation. Without faith it is impossible to please God (Hebrews 11:6). Therefore, it is of paramount importance that we as parents live by faith in relation to such issues as our health, our responsibility in the home and church, our financial obligations, and the normal stresses of life. A joyful trusting in God for daily strength and wisdom says much to the child about the indispensable element of faith.

Issues Related to Parenting

9. *Gratitude*

Teaching your child to be grateful for all that he has and all that he receives is a virtue of lasting worth. The Scriptures give a vivid account of how unholiness always follows unthankfulness (Romans 1:21–32; 2 Timothy 3:1–7). Therefore, it matters much that the child be taught to say "thank you" and to sense appreciation for the many favors he receives daily from the hands of others.

Jesus' example of thanking God for the five loaves and two fishes and His calling attention to the one leper out of ten should help us appreciate the importance of gratitude.

When a parent expresses faith in the fact that God is all-in-all, that He is all powerful, all wise, all good, all loving, and in control of everything, the child can rest in gratefulness that all his needs will be supplied. A child who feels grateful for his present circumstances will also know contentment and happiness.

Gratefulness also helps one to experience joy even in difficult times. Knowing

Character Development

that happiness and peace do not depend on congenial external circumstances but on a right understanding of God's providence helps the child to be grateful even in the face of adversity.

Being grateful will not only contribute to a contented life that is free from covetousness, but will also help the child to escape many sinful perversions. Rather than lustfully pursuing fleshly passions, the child can be taught the blessing of thanking God for his body and its functions and surrendering it all for His glory.

10. Cautiousness

The Bible warns of the danger of acting impulsively, of acting without thinking a situation through. "He that hasteth with his feet sinneth" (Proverbs 19:2). Without a sense of cautiousness, an individual can rush into a bad or dangerous situation. Cautiousness means being careful to do the right thing in the right time and in the right way.

Issues Related to Parenting

Carefulness is the quality of thoughtfully evaluating the possible consequences of decisions and actions before one acts. Cautiousness involves learning that unfamiliar situations may contain danger. It seeks advice and counsel before making decisions. It is the ability to see future consequences of present actions and decisions. Cautiousness also involves learning how to detect and avoid evil associations, as well as recognizing and fleeing temptation.

The child must be trained to be cautious. However, while helping the child develop a sense of caution, the parent must be careful not to generate unnecessary fears. A wolf is not lurking behind every tree, and certainly not every new, unseen circumstance poses a potential threat to the child's physical or moral well-being.

Developing cautiousness in a child starts with warnings concerning dangers in the house—the hot stove, hot water, sharp objects. The child who ignores these warnings

Character Development

will experience pain. Valuable lessons are learned by firsthand experience, but generally they are costly. Learning cautiousness in the home from both warning and experience will help the child avoid greater potential dangers outside the home.

Growing up, children will encounter a variety of temptations. The most dangerous are the sugar-coated ones—those that are accompanied by such challenges from the crowd as:

> "How can you know if you don't try it?"
> "A little bit never hurt anyone."
> "We'll be careful to stop in time."
> "Don't be a 'fraidy cat."
> "No one will ever know."

Such arguments should send up red warning flags to the child or young person who has been trained to be cautious.

The blatant moral perversion of free love and sex is the result of throwing all caution to the wind. In the home the child must be taught to flee any person or temptation that would encourage him to experiment with or

Issues Related to Parenting

gratify sensual impulse. Helping children develop the character trait of cautiousness in this area will help them avoid many other pitfalls and tragedies throughout life.

11. Patience

As well as training the child to be cautious, the parent also needs to teach patience. Patience is learning how to wait contentedly for the fulfillment of personal desires, wants, and goals. When a child learns patience, he also learns that God has a time for everything (Ecclesiastes 3:1–8). Such knowledge conditions him to understand in later years that it is for our personal benefit to wait upon God to fulfill His will in our lives.

Wanting something "right now" has led many people, especially the young, into many hurtful paths of sin. Entering into courtship prematurely and pursuing the urge to pet and caress have prompted many people to commit fornication and scar their lives.

Buying merchandise on credit has also led

Character Development

many to financial bondage. Patience will teach us not only to learn to earn and save money before making purchases, but also to be willing to live without luxuries.

Patience is also reflected in good driving habits, for example, choosing to drive within the speed limit, observing and obeying road signs, and giving the other driver the benefit and advantage. Many accidents would be avoided if the Scripture "Let patience have her perfect work" (James 1:4) were followed.

Parents can help their children develop patience by not allowing them to eat between meals, by letting them reap the results of their own mistakes, by teaching them some skills, and by making them wait until they are sufficiently mature to date or drive. Children will also learn from the parents' own example. Seeing their parents sacrifice time and luxuries and wait upon God to meet their needs will act as an incentive to them to do the same. This is especially true when the parents demonstrate a happy, thankful,

Issues Related to Parenting

joyful, and contented spirit while trusting and waiting.

12. Security

Having looked at eleven basic traits of character, we will conclude with one more—a sense of security. To avoid fears, to achieve in school, to maintain a good digestive system, to sleep peacefully, and much more, children need to experience security.

True security ultimately stems from the knowledge that God is all-powerful, all-knowing, all-caring, and all-wise. It comes from the faith that believes that God will take care of us even when external circumstances seem to show otherwise. Naturally, the child is not born with this sense of security. Therefore, it becomes the parents' urgent responsibility to provide such a sheltered environment that will give the child this trust.

This trust and security will develop as children see and sense that their parents have built their hope for the future on the promises

Character Development

of God rather than on material possessions, their own abilities, job security or pension plans, and personal savings, all of which can be taken away.

Security is also developed as parents provide proper shelter, food, and clothing. When a child has these essentials provided and is surrounded by love, he can feel secure even when normal situations and schedules are disrupted.

Affection and harmony between father and mother provide the child with a further basis for security. Then as he feels this love overshadowing him in spite of his worthiness or unworthiness, he also can become a stable factor in the lives of his peers.

As children grow older, parents should work to transfer the basis of the child's security from themselves to the Lord. This can only be done as parents help and lead their children to an experience of true repentance—a repentance that confesses and believes that nothing of saving merit exists

Issues Related to Parenting

in one's own character; a repentance that embraces faith and confidence in the Lord of glory as the only one who can lead a person from where he is to where the Lord wants him to be.

In summary: The work of parenting is never finished. Character traits that were not discussed—such as meekness, diligence, punctuality, thriftiness, dependability, determination, flexibility, generosity, and loyalty—all add to the development of a child who can be of greater use in the kingdom of God.

Parental example in all the character traits mentioned is immeasurably important and valuable. Our children are largely what we as parents are. Their actions often mirror our own character. The more we express the divine nature and character of our Lord Jesus Christ, the greater will the advantage be to our children.

In this perilous and permissive age, let us as parents rise up and shoulder the responsibility and the privilege that are ours, so that the generation that follows us may be able to say, "Thank You, Lord, for parents who loved me, cared for me, and brought me up in the nurture and admonition of the Lord."

Chapter 7, with some revision, is taken from *Growing Up God's Way* by John A. Stomer.
Used by permission of Liberty Press.